I0416713

FROM PROSPECT TO PROFIT: THE COMPLETE GUIDE TO SALES AND MARKETING FUSION

THANK YOU, LORD JESUS, FOR THE COUNTLESS BLESSINGS OF HAPPINESS, PEACE, AND PROSPERITY THAT GRACE MY DAYS!

FOR RAJI, ALEN & HELEN

CONTENTS

PREFACE

Welcome to our journey together through "From Prospect to Profit: The Complete Guide to Sales and Marketing Fusion." This book is more than a collection of strategies and insights; it reflects my journey through the evolving landscapes of sales and marketing. As someone who has navigated the choppy waters of aligning teams, embracing new technologies, and striving to understand the ever-changing desires of customers, I've learned that the fusion of sales and marketing isn't just a strategic necessity—it's a transformative opportunity to forge deeper connections with our customers and drive meaningful growth.

The genesis of this book was sparked by a simple yet profound realisation: the traditional divide between sales and marketing teams is a barrier to success in today's digitally driven, customer-centric world. This realisation came not from reading articles or attending conferences and webinars but from the trenches—working day in and day out with teams striving to reach their customers in more impactful ways.

As we dive into the following pages, I invite you to view each chapter as a book segment and a milestone in a shared journey, from the evolution of sales and marketing as separate disciplines to the seamless integration that today's market demands, we'll explore how aligning our efforts can create extraordinary customer experiences and drive our businesses forward.

This guide is crafted for you—whether you are a sales professional seeking to understand the nuances of modern marketing, a marketer looking to align more closely with sales objectives, or a business leader aiming to cultivate a culture of collaboration and innovation. I hope that within these pages, you will find inspiration, practical advice, and the occasional moment of clarity that transforms your approach to sales and marketing.

The journey from prospect to profit is filled with challenges, surprises, and growth opportunities. It requires us to be relentless learners, empathetic communicators, and bold experimenters. As we embark on this journey together, I am excited to share the lessons I have learned, the mistakes I have made, and the successes from embracing the fusion of sales and marketing.

Thank you for picking up this book and being willing to explore new possibilities for your sales and marketing efforts. Here's to our journey together, from prospect to profit.

Warm Regards!
Shanty Abraham

CHAPTER 1: INTRODUCTION TO SALES AND MARKETING FUSION

In the dynamic business world, sales and marketing have long been recognised as vital components of organisational success. Traditionally operating in silos, these functions have embarked on a journey towards closer integration and collaboration. This chapter delves into the evolution of sales and marketing as separate entities and their convergence into a unified force. This approach has come to be known as the fusion of sales and marketing.

The Evolution of Sales and Marketing
Historically, Sales and marketing have been viewed as distinct disciplines, each with a unique focus, strategy, and objectives. Marketing was primarily concerned with building brand awareness, generating leads, and establishing a market presence through advertising, product promotion, and public relations. Its strategies were designed to appeal to a broad audience and create interest and desire for products or services.

On the other hand, sales focused on converting prospects into customers through direct interactions, negotiations, and closing deals. Sales strategies were personalised, targeting specific individuals or organisations with tailored solutions to meet their unique needs.

Despite their different approaches, both sales and marketing shared the goal of driving revenue and business growth. However, the lack of integration often led to missed opportunities, inefficiencies, and sometimes conflicting objectives.

Understanding the Fusion: Sales Meets Marketing

The digital revolution has dramatically transformed the business landscape, altering how companies engage with customers and conduct operations. This transformation has necessitated a closer alignment between sales and marketing, leading to what is now known as their fusion.

The fusion of sales and marketing is characterised by a strategic alignment where both departments work closely together towards common goals. This collaboration is facilitated by shared information, coordinated efforts, and a unified approach to customer engagement. The fusion aims to create a seamless customer experience from the initial point of contact through the entire buyer's journey, culminating in the conversion and beyond.

Several factors have contributed to the fusion of sales and marketing:

1. **Customer Empowerment**: Today's customers are more informed and have higher expectations. They demand consistent, personalised interactions across all touchpoints. Sales and marketing fusion ensures that messaging and engagement are coherent and tailored to the customer's stage in the buying journey.

2. **Data and Technology**: Advances in technology, especially in data analytics and customer relationship management (CRM) systems, have provided the tools necessary for sales and marketing to align closely.

These tools offer insights into customer behaviour, preferences, and engagement history, enabling more effective targeting and personalization.

3. **Content Marketing**: The rise of content marketing has blurred the lines between sales and marketing. High-quality, relevant content is used not just to attract prospects but also to nurture them through the sales funnel. This requires a coordinated effort to ensure that content meets the needs of potential customers at every stage.

4. **Performance Metrics**: The fusion of sales and marketing also involves a shift in measuring success. Instead of focusing on separate metrics, such as leads generated (marketing) and deals closed (sales), organisations are adopting integrated metrics that reflect the health and effectiveness of the entire funnel, such as customer acquisition cost (CAC) and lifetime value (LTV).

The fusion of sales and marketing has its challenges. It requires a cultural shift, open communication, and the breaking down of traditional silos. However, when successfully implemented, it leads to enhanced efficiency, improved customer satisfaction, and, ultimately, increased revenue and business growth.

As we explore the nuances of this fusion in the following sections, we will uncover the strategies, technologies, and best practices that have enabled leading organisations to seamlessly integrate their sales and marketing efforts, setting a new standard for business operations in the digital age.

CHAPTER 2: THE FOUNDATIONS OF FUSION

The fusion of sales and marketing represents more than a strategic realignment of two business functions. It embodies a fundamental shift towards a more integrated, customer-centric approach. This chapter explores the foundational elements necessary for successfully merging sales and marketing efforts, focusing on building a customer-centric approach, understanding the psychology behind buying decisions, and crafting a compelling value proposition.

Building a Customer-Centric Approach
A customer-centric approach places the customer at the heart of every business decision and action. This approach is crucial for the fusion of sales and marketing, as it ensures that both departments are aligned to meet and exceed customer expectations. Implementing a customer-centric approach involves several key steps:

1. **Deep Customer Understanding**: This involves gathering and analysing data on customer behaviours, preferences, needs, and pain points. Advanced analytics, customer feedback, and direct interactions are invaluable for gaining these insights.

2. **Segmentation and Personalisation**: Armed with

deep customer insights, businesses can segment their audience into distinct groups with similar characteristics and tailor their marketing and sales strategies to address the specific needs of each segment.

3. **Customer Journey Mapping**: Understanding the customer's journey from awareness to purchase and beyond is critical. This enables sales and marketing to align their efforts to provide the right touchpoints and messages at each journey stage.

4. **Feedback Loops**: Establishing mechanisms for continuous customer feedback allows businesses to adapt and refine their strategies, ensuring that they remain customer centric.

The Psychology Behind Buying Decisions

Understanding the psychological factors influencing buying decisions is essential for effectively integrating sales and marketing strategies. Several psychological principles play a crucial role in how customers make purchasing decisions:

1. **Emotional Appeal**: Purchases are often driven by emotions, such as desire, fear, or happiness before being justified by logic. Crafting messages that resonate emotionally can significantly impact buying behavior.

2. **Social Proof**: Buyers are influenced by the actions and opinions of others. Testimonials, reviews, and endorsements can leverage social proof to build trust and credibility.

3. **Authority**: Establishing authority and expertise in your industry can influence buying decisions. Providing valuable insights, thought leadership and

evidence-based benefits can help sway potential customers.

4. **Scarcity and Urgency**: The perception of scarcity or a limited-time offer can create a sense of urgency, prompting quicker decision-making.

Understanding these psychological triggers can help sales and marketing create more effective campaigns and interactions that align with the buyer's mindset.

Crafting Your Value Proposition

The value proposition is a clear statement that explains how a product or service solves a customer's problem or improves their situation. It delivers specific benefits and tells the ideal customer why they should buy from you and not from the competition. A compelling value proposition is critical for combining sales and marketing, providing a unified message that both departments can communicate.

To craft a compelling value proposition, consider the following:

1. **Identify Customer Benefits**: Focus on the benefits that truly matter to your customers. These can include functional benefits, such as time savings or cost reductions, and emotional benefits, such as feeling secure or prosperous.

2. **Differentiate from Competitors**: Clearly articulate

what makes your offering unique and why it's a better choice than others in the market.

3. **Use Clear and Concise Language**: Your value proposition should be easily understood and compelling. Avoid jargon and complex terms that might confuse potential customers.

4. **Test and Refine**: Your value proposition is not set in stone. It should evolve based on customer feedback, market changes, and competitive dynamics. Continuously testing and refining your value proposition ensures it remains relevant and compelling.

The foundations of sales and marketing fusion—building a customer-centric approach, understanding the psychology behind buying decisions, and crafting a compelling value proposition—are integral to creating a seamless and effective strategy that drives growth and customer loyalty. As organisations navigate the complexities of the modern marketplace, these foundational elements provide the guidance necessary to achieve a successful fusion of sales and marketing efforts.

CHAPTER 3: DATA-DRIVEN STRATEGIES

In the era of sales and marketing fusion, leveraging data-driven strategies is a cornerstone for achieving alignment and maximising effectiveness. This chapter delves into the pivotal role of analytics in harmonising sales and marketing efforts, the nuances of customer segmentation and targeting, and the transformative impact of predictive analytics on forecasting sales trends.

Leveraging Analytics for Sales and Marketing Alignment
Integrating analytics into sales and marketing strategies offers unparalleled insights into customer behaviours, preferences, and engagement patterns. By harnessing the power of data analytics, organisations can achieve a higher degree of alignment between sales and marketing, leading to more effective customer acquisition and retention strategies. Key aspects include:

1. **Unified Data Platform**: Establishing a unified data platform ensures that sales and marketing access the same data sets, facilitating a shared understanding of customer dynamics and enabling coordinated strategies.

2. **Performance Measurement**: Analytics enables the measurement of key performance indicators (KPIs) across sales and marketing, allowing for a comprehensive assessment of campaign effectiveness,

lead generation, conversion rates, and ROI.

3. **Customer Insights**: Data analytics provides deep insights into customer behaviour and preferences, informing content creation, messaging, and engagement strategies that resonate with the target audience.

4. **Optimisation**: Continuous data analysis allows for optimising sales and marketing tactics in real-time, adjusting strategies based on customer responses and market changes.

Customer Segmentation and Targeting Techniques

Effective customer segmentation and targeting are fundamental to maximising the impact of sales and marketing efforts. By dividing the customer base into distinct groups based on shared characteristics or behaviours, organisations can tailor their approaches to address each segment's specific needs and preferences. Advanced targeting techniques involve:

1. **Demographic Segmentation**: This involves categorising customers based on age, gender, income, education, and other demographic factors to tailor products and marketing messages.

2. **Behavioural Segmentation**: Segmenting customers based on their purchasing behaviour, website interactions, and engagement with marketing materials enables highly personalised marketing and sales strategies.

3. **Geographic Segmentation**: Target customers based on location to deliver region-specific messages and offers.

4. **Psychographic Segmentation**: Understanding customers' lifestyles, values, and attitudes to create

more emotionally resonant and compelling marketing campaigns.

Predictive Analytics in Forecasting Sales Trends

Predictive analytics harnesses historical data, statistical algorithms, and machine learning techniques to forecast future sales trends. This predictive approach enables sales and marketing teams to anticipate market shifts, customer needs, and potential opportunities or challenges before they arise. Key applications include:

1. **Sales Forecasting**: Predictive models analyse past sales data and market trends to forecast future sales performance, helping organisations allocate resources effectively and set realistic targets.

2. **Lead Scoring**: Predictive analytics are utilised to score leads based on their likelihood to convert, enabling sales teams to prioritise high-potential leads and tailor their outreach strategies accordingly.

3. **Customer Lifetime Value Prediction** involves estimating customers' future value to identify high-value segments and tailor retention strategies to maximise long-term profitability.

4. **Churn Prediction** involves identifying signals that a customer is likely to churn, allowing preemptive action to retain them through targeted offers or engagement strategies.

Data-driven strategies are the lifeblood of modern sales and marketing fusion. They empower organisations to make informed decisions, tailor their approaches to meet the unique needs of their customer base and anticipate market trends. By embracing analytics, customer segmentation, and predictive modelling, businesses can navigate the complexities of the marketplace with agility and precision, driving sustainable growth and competitive advantage.

CHAPTER 4:
CONTENT IS KING:
MARKETING FOR
SALES ENABLEMENT

In the digital age, content has emerged as a dominant force in the intersection of sales and marketing. High-quality, relevant content attracts and engages potential customers and plays a crucial role in converting leads into sales. This chapter explores the art of creating content that sells, leveraging video marketing for engagement and conversion, and utilising social media to nurture leads, ultimately enhancing sales enablement.

Creating Content That Sells: Blogs, Whitepapers, and Case Studies

Effective content marketing involves strategically creating and distributing valuable, relevant, and consistent content to attract and retain a clearly defined audience — and, ultimately, to drive profitable customer action. To achieve this, several content formats stand out for their ability to inform, persuade, and convert.

1. **Blogs**: Blogs are an accessible platform for sharing insights, industry news, and solutions to common problems. They help establish authority and trust while boosting search engine visibility and drawing

more traffic to your website.

2. **Whitepapers**: Whitepapers are in-depth reports on specific topics that present a problem and provide a solution. They are excellent tools for lead generation, as they often require an exchange of contact information for access.

3. **Case Studies**: Case studies are real-world examples of how your product or service successfully addresses a customer's needs. They provide tangible proof of your value proposition and can significantly influence purchasing decisions by showcasing your offerings' practical application and benefits.

Video Marketing: A Tool for Engagement and Conversion

Video marketing has become a powerful tool for captivating audiences, conveying messages dynamically, and driving engagement and conversion. Its effectiveness lies in its ability to humanise brands, demonstrate products in action, and tell stories that resonate with viewers on an emotional level.

1. **Product Demos**: Video demonstrations that showcase how your product works and its benefits can help demystify complex offerings and persuade potential customers of their value.

2. **Testimonials**: Customer testimonials in video format offer a genuine, relatable, and persuasive perspective that can boost credibility and trust among prospects.

3. **Explainer Videos**: These videos provide clear and concise explanations of products or concepts, making them particularly useful for breaking complex information into digestible, engaging content.

Utilizing Social Media to Nurture Leads

Social media platforms are invaluable for nurturing leads through personalised engagement and targeted content. They offer a direct line to potential customers, enabling real-time communication and fostering community around your brand.

1. **Targeted Advertising**: Social media platforms offer advanced targeting options, allowing you to deliver ads to specific demographics, interests, and behaviours, thus increasing the likelihood of engagement and conversion.

2. **Content Sharing**: Sharing a mix of blogs, whitepapers, case studies, and videos on social media can drive traffic to your website and keep your audience engaged with your brand.

3. **Community Building**: Engaging with users, responding to comments, and conversing to build relationships with potential customers. Creating a community around your brand can lead to higher loyalty and advocacy.

Content, in its various forms, is a cornerstone of modern marketing strategies and a key sales enabler. By creating content that educates, engages, and convinces, leveraging the dynamic appeal of video, and utilising the expansive reach of social media, organisations can effectively nurture leads through the sales funnel. The fusion of content marketing with sales strategies not only enhances lead generation and conversion rates but also establishes a lasting relationship with customers, reinforcing the notion that content is truly king.

CHAPTER 5: DIGITAL MARKETING TACTICS FOR SALES GROWTH

In an increasingly digital world, businesses must leverage online channels to drive sales growth effectively. This chapter explores the pivotal digital marketing tactics that align with sales objectives, focusing on Search Engine Optimization (SEO) and Search Engine Marketing (SEM), email marketing strategies for lead nurturing, and the strategic use of Pay-Per-Click (PPC) campaigns. These tactics are not standalone but interwoven strategies that, when executed cohesively, can significantly enhance a company's sales performance.

SEO and SEM: Capturing Intent and Driving Traffic
SEO and SEM are foundational components of a digital marketing strategy, designed to increase visibility in search engine results and capture user intent at critical moments.

- **SEO**: SEO involves optimising website content, structure, and on-page elements like keywords, meta descriptions, and title tags, along with off-page factors such as backlinks, to rank higher in organic search results. The goal is to attract quality traffic to your site by ensuring that your content aligns with the queries your target audience is searching for. This long-term strategy builds credibility and trust with potential customers, making it easier to convert them into leads and sales.

- **SEM**: SEM uses paid advertising to increase visibility in search engine results pages (SERPs). Through platforms like Google Ads, businesses can create ads that appear to users actively searching for related keywords. SEM allows for precise targeting and immediate visibility, making it a powerful tool for driving targeted traffic and capturing leads who have a high intent to purchase.

SEO and SEM provide a comprehensive approach to capturing user intent, driving traffic, and, ultimately, enhancing sales growth.

Email Marketing Strategies for Lead Nurturing

Email marketing remains one of the most effective digital marketing tactics for building relationships with leads and guiding them through the sales funnel.

- **Segmentation and Personalisation**: To maximise the effectiveness of email marketing, segment your audience based on their behaviours, preferences, and where they are in the buyer's journey. Tailor your emails to their needs and interests, making the content relevant and engaging.

- **Value-Driven Content**: Emails should provide value, whether in the form of educational content, exclusive offers, or updates on products and services. This approach helps build trust and credibility with your audience, making them more likely to convert into paying customers.

- **Automation and Drip Campaigns**: Utilise automation tools to send timely, relevant emails based on specific triggers, such as a user signing up for your newsletter or downloading a whitepaper. Drip campaigns can nurture leads by providing them with a steady stream of valuable information, gently guiding them towards making a purchase.

Pay-Per-Click (PPC) Campaigns: Maximising ROI

PPC campaigns offer a direct route to gaining visibility and driving targeted traffic to your website. The advantage is that you pay only when someone clicks on your ad.

- **Targeted Advertising**: PPC platforms offer sophisticated targeting options, including keywords, demographics, interests, and behaviours, allowing you to reach your ideal customers with precision.
- **Measurable Results**: With PPC, every aspect of your campaign can be measured, from the number of clicks to conversions. This data enables you to assess the effectiveness of your ads and make informed decisions to optimise your campaigns for better ROI.

- **Flexibility and Control**: PPC campaigns can be adjusted in real-time based on performance data, market trends, or changes in business strategy. This flexibility ensures you can continuously align your advertising efforts with your sales objectives.

- **Landing Pages**: To maximise the effectiveness of your PPC campaigns, direct traffic to dedicated landing pages that are optimised for conversion. These pages should provide a clear value proposition, persuasive copy, and a straightforward call to action (CTA).

Digital marketing tactics such as SEO, SEM, email marketing, and PPC campaigns are essential tools in the modern marketer's arsenal for driving sales growth. By leveraging these strategies effectively, businesses can improve their online visibility, engage with their target audience, and guide potential customers through the sales funnel, ultimately leading to increased sales and revenue.

CHAPTER 6: THE SALES PROCESS REDEFINED

The traditional sales process has undergone significant transformation in the contemporary business landscape. This metamorphosis reflects the evolving market dynamics, customer expectations, and the integration of technology into every aspect of sales activities. To remain effective, today's sales professionals must adapt by refining their approach to communication, negotiation, closing techniques, and post-sale engagement. This chapter explores these critical aspects, offering insights into redefining the sales process for today's market.

Effective Communication and Negotiation Skills

Effective communication is the foundation of any successful sales process, extending beyond verbal exchanges to digital interactions. Sales professionals must be adept at conveying value, understanding customer needs, and building relationships across multiple platforms, including email, social media, and virtual meetings.

- **Active Listening** involves hearing, understanding, and responding to customer concerns and questions, demonstrating empathy, and building trust.

- **Clear and Concise Messaging**: With the overload of information, sales messages must be clear, concise, and compelling to capture attention and convey value quickly.

- **Adaptive Communication Styles**: Sales professionals

should adapt their communication style to match their customer's preferences, whether formal or informal, detailed, or high-level, to enhance rapport and engagement.

Negotiation skills are equally crucial, as they enable sales professionals to navigate objections, find mutually beneficial solutions, and secure commitments without compromising on value.

- **Win-Win Outcomes**: Focus on negotiation strategies that seek win-win outcomes, emphasising the value proposition and aligning it with customer needs.

- **Flexibility and Creativity**: Flexibility and creativity in negotiations can help overcome barriers, whether through customised solutions, payment plans, or additional services.

Closing Techniques That Work in Today's Market

Closing the sale is often the most challenging part, requiring a delicate balance of persuasion, timing, and technique. The following are effective closing techniques tailored for today's market:

- **The Assumptive Close**: This technique assumes the sale has been made and moves forward with the following steps, such as discussing payment plans or delivery schedules. It's based on positive momentum and the strength of the sales dialogue.

- **The Consultative Close**: Here, the sales professional acts more as a consultant than a traditional salesperson, making recommendations based on a deep understanding of the customer's business challenges and goals. This approach builds trust and positions the sales professional as a valuable partner.

- **The Incentive Close**: Offering a time-sensitive incentive can create a sense of urgency, encouraging the customer to decide. However, incentives must be used sparingly and strategically to avoid diminishing the perceived value of the offering.

Post-Sale: Building Loyalty and Encouraging Referrals

The sales process does not end with the close; in many ways, it's just the beginning of a longer relationship-building journey. Post-sale engagement is essential for building loyalty, encouraging repeat business, and generating referrals.

- **Follow-Up and Support**: Regular follow-ups ensure that customers are satisfied with their purchase and help identify any issues or opportunities for additional sales.

- **Customer Appreciation**: Showing appreciation through thank-you notes, personalised offers, or customer appreciation events can deepen relationships and enhance loyalty.

- **Referral Programs**: Encouraging satisfied customers to refer others can be an effective way to generate new leads. Referral programs should offer incentives that are valuable to your customers and easy to participate in.

Redefining the sales process for today's market involves a holistic approach encompassing effective communication, modern closing techniques, and a strong focus on post-sale engagement. By adapting to these evolved strategies, sales professionals can better meet the needs of contemporary customers, driving success in an ever-changing sales environment.

CHAPTER 7: INTEGRATING TECHNOLOGY INTO SALES AND MARKETING

Integrating technology into sales and marketing strategies has revolutionised how businesses approach customer engagement, lead management, and personalisation. This chapter explores the transformative role of Customer Relationship Management (CRM) systems, marketing automation tools, and the innovative applications of Artificial Intelligence (AI) and Machine Learning (ML) in refining sales and marketing efforts for enhanced performance and customer satisfaction.

CRM Systems: Tracking Prospects to Profit

CRM systems stand at the core of modern sales and marketing integration, providing a unified platform for tracking customer interactions, managing leads, and analysing sales pipelines. These systems facilitate a seamless flow of information between sales and marketing teams, ensuring that both are aligned to convert prospects into profitable customers. Key benefits include:

- **Centralised Data Management**: CRM systems centralise customer data, making it accessible to sales and marketing teams, thus enhancing collaboration and ensuring a unified approach to customer engagement.

- **Lead Management**: CRM systems enable sales teams to nurture leads more effectively, prioritise follow-ups based on lead scoring, and close deals more efficiently by tracking every interaction with prospects.

- **Sales Forecasting**: Advanced CRM solutions provide tools for detailed sales forecasting, allowing businesses to predict future sales trends, set realistic targets, and allocate resources more efficiently.

- **Customer Insights**: CRM analytics offer deep insights into customer behaviour and preferences, helping sales and marketing teams tailor their strategies to meet the specific needs of their target audience.

Marketing Automation: Streamlining Your Sales Funnel

Marketing automation technology has become an indispensable tool for streamlining sales and marketing processes, automating repetitive tasks, and delivering personalised customer experiences at scale. Implementing marketing automation yields several advantages:

- **Efficient Lead Generation**: Automation tools can capture leads across various channels, segment them based on predefined criteria, and feed them into the sales funnel, increasing the efficiency of lead generation efforts.

- **Personalised Communication**: By automating email campaigns, social media posts, and targeted advertisements, businesses can maintain consistent and personalised communication with their audience, enhancing engagement and conversion rates.

- **Campaign Management**: Marketing automation platforms enable the design, execution, and measurement of marketing campaigns, providing insights into their performance and facilitating continuous optimisation.

- **Resource Optimisation**: By automating routine tasks, businesses can allocate their resources more effectively, focusing on strategic planning and creative tasks that require human input.

The Role of AI and Machine Learning in Personalization

AI and ML technologies are pushing the boundaries of personalisation in sales and marketing, enabling businesses to deliver highly personalised customer experiences based on predictive insights and real-time data analysis.

- **Predictive Analytics**: AI-driven predictive analytics can forecast customer behaviour, purchase likelihood, and potential churn, allowing sales and marketing teams to address customer needs and preferences proactively.
- **Dynamic Content Personalisation**: AI algorithms can dynamically personalise website content, email messages, and product recommendations for each visitor, significantly improving the relevance and effectiveness of marketing efforts.

- **Chatbots and Virtual Assistants**: AI-powered chatbots and virtual assistants provide 24/7 customer service, answering queries, assisting with purchases, and guiding customers through the sales funnel without human intervention.

- **Customer Sentiment Analysis**: ML algorithms can analyse customer feedback, social media comments, and online reviews to gauge sentiment and identify trends, enabling businesses to adjust their strategies in response to customer perceptions and needs.

The integration of technology into sales and marketing enhances operational efficiency and provides unprecedented opportunities for personalisation, engagement, and customer insight. By leveraging CRM systems, marketing automation, and AI/ML technologies, businesses can create a cohesive, data-driven strategy that aligns sales and marketing efforts, drives growth, and delivers exceptional customer experiences.

CHAPTER 8:
OVERCOMING
CHALLENGES IN SALES
AND MARKETING
FUSION

Integrating sales and marketing functions marks a transformative step toward achieving organisational synergy and enhanced customer experiences. However, this fusion has its challenges. From cultural differences and misaligned objectives to the complexities of data management, organisations must navigate various obstacles to realise the full potential of this integration. This chapter explores the challenges faced in sales and marketing fusion, strategies for aligning teams towards common goals, and the importance of continuous improvement through metrics and feedback.

Identifying and Addressing Common Roadblocks

Several roadblocks can hinder the effective fusion of sales and marketing teams. Identifying and proactively addressing these challenges is crucial for smooth integration.

- **Cultural Differences**: Sales and marketing teams often have distinct cultures and workstyles, leading to misunderstandings and friction. Bridging this gap requires open communication, shared experiences, and team-building activities that foster mutual respect and understanding.

- **Data Silos**: Disjointed data management systems can prevent teams from accessing shared insights, leading to duplicated efforts, and missed opportunities. Implementing integrated CRM and marketing automation platforms can help break down these silos, ensuring everyone has access to the same data.

- **Misaligned Objectives**: When sales and marketing have different goals or success metrics, it can lead to conflicting strategies. Establishing shared objectives and KPIs is essential for aligning efforts and fostering a sense of shared purpose.

Aligning Teams Towards Common Goals

Achieving alignment between sales and marketing teams is foundational to overcoming integration challenges. The following strategies can facilitate this alignment:

- **Joint Planning and Goal Setting**: Involving both teams in planning and setting common goals can help align strategies and expectations. This collaborative approach ensures that both teams are working towards the same objectives.

- **Cross-Functional Teams**: Creating cross-functional teams or task forces for specific projects or campaigns can improve collaboration and communication. These teams can be integration champions, promoting fusion benefits across both departments.

- **Regular Communication**: Establishing regular check-ins, updates, and feedback sessions between sales and marketing teams can enhance transparency and foster a culture of collaboration. Communication channels should be open and accessible to all team members.

Continuous Improvement: Learning from Metrics and Feedback

The fusion of sales and marketing is an ongoing process

that requires continuous evaluation and adaptation. Leveraging metrics and feedback is critical to identifying areas for improvement and driving innovation.

- **Metrics and Analytics**: Implementing a data-driven approach to monitor the performance of sales and marketing activities is crucial. Analysing metrics such as lead conversion rates, customer acquisition costs, and customer lifetime value can provide insights into the effectiveness of integration efforts.

- **Feedback Loops**: Establishing mechanisms for collecting and acting on feedback from teams and customers can guide continuous improvement. This feedback can highlight areas of friction, uncover new opportunities, and inform strategy adjustments.

- **Innovation and Experimentation**: Encouraging a culture of innovation and allowing teams to experiment with new strategies or technologies can lead to sales and marketing effectiveness breakthroughs. Learning from both successes and failures is essential for growth and adaptation.

Overcoming the challenges in sales and marketing fusion requires a strategic approach focused on alignment, communication, and continuous improvement. By addressing common roadblocks, fostering collaboration, and leveraging insights from metrics and feedback, organisations can enhance their sales and marketing integration, driving improved performance and customer satisfaction.

CHAPTER 9: FUTURE TRENDS IN SALES AND MARKETING

As we navigate the ever-evolving landscape of sales and marketing, staying ahead requires a keen eye on emerging trends and the ability to adapt swiftly to market changes. Moreover, the growing importance of sustainability and ethical practices in business operations is reshaping the strategies of sales and marketing teams worldwide. This chapter explores the future trends in sales and marketing, focusing on the impact of emerging technologies, methods for adapting to market changes, and the significance of building sustainable and ethical practices.

Emerging Technologies and Their Impact
The role of technology in transforming sales and marketing strategies cannot be overstated. From artificial intelligence (AI) and machine learning (ML) to augmented reality (AR) and blockchain, emerging technologies are setting the stage for a new era of customer engagement and business operations.

- **Artificial Intelligence and Machine Learning**: AI and ML are revolutionising sales and marketing by enabling personalised customer experiences at scale, optimising marketing campaigns, and providing predictive insights that drive decision-making.

- **Augmented Reality**: AR technology enhances the customer experience by allowing consumers to visualise products in their environment before purchasing, bridging the gap between online and physical shopping experiences.

- **Blockchain**: Blockchain technology is emerging as a tool for enhancing transparency and security in transactions. It could potentially transform how customer data is stored and shared and create new paradigms for customer trust.

- **Internet of Things (IoT)**: IoT devices are collecting vast amounts of data that can be leveraged to understand customer behaviour, preferences, and needs, enabling more targeted and timely marketing strategies.

Staying Ahead: Adapting to Market Changes

Adapting to market changes is crucial for staying competitive in the fast-paced world of sales and marketing. Organisations must cultivate agility and foster a culture of continuous learning to navigate the challenges and opportunities that arise from market dynamics.

- **Continuous Learning and Skill Development**: Encouraging constant learning and professional development within teams ensures that your organisation remains at the cutting edge of sales and marketing strategies.

- **Agile Marketing**: Adopting agile marketing methodologies allows teams to respond more to market changes, test new ideas quickly, and iterate based on feedback and results.

- **Customer-centricity**: It is essential to stay relevant and competitive to maintain a deep understanding of your customers and be responsive to their changing needs and preferences.

Building Sustainable and Ethical Sales and Marketing Practices

As consumers become more conscious of environmental and ethical issues, businesses are increasingly pressured to adopt sustainable and ethical practices. This shift affects not only how products are made but also how they are marketed and sold.

- **Transparency**: Consumers demand transparency in how products are sourced, manufactured, and marketed. Sales and marketing teams must ensure that their practices meet these expectations and communicate them effectively to consumers.
- **Ethical Marketing**: Marketing strategies should be built on moral principles, avoiding misleading claims and respecting consumer privacy. This creates long-term trust and loyalty among customers.

- **Sustainability**: Integrating sustainability into the sales and marketing strategy is becoming necessary. This includes promoting eco-friendly products, reducing waste in marketing materials, and leveraging digital channels to minimise the environmental footprint.

The future of sales and marketing lies in integrating emerging technologies, swiftly adapting to market changes, and committing to sustainable and ethical practices. By focusing on these areas, organisations can stay ahead of the curve and build a loyal customer base that values their approach to business and the environment.

CHAPTER 10: CASE STUDIES AND SUCCESS STORIES

The fusion of sales and marketing strategies represents a paradigm shift in how businesses approach customer engagement and drive growth. This chapter delves into real-world examples of successful sales and marketing integration, offering insights and lessons learned from industry leaders. These case studies illustrate the transformative impact of aligning sales and marketing efforts, showcasing the strategies, challenges, and outcomes experienced by companies across various sectors.

Real-World Examples of Sales and Marketing Fusion
Tech Giant: Salesforce

Strategy: Salesforce is renowned for its customer-centric approach. It leverages its CRM platform to bridge the gap between sales and marketing. The company employs a unified data model that allows sales and marketing to share insights and collaborate more effectively.

Outcome: This strategic alignment has enabled Salesforce to provide personalised customer experiences at a scale, significantly improving lead conversion rates and customer satisfaction. The company's consistent growth and market leadership underscore the effectiveness of its integrated approach.

E-commerce Leader: Amazon

Strategy: Amazon uses sophisticated data analytics and machine learning algorithms to align its sales and marketing efforts. Amazon delivers highly personalised product recommendations and marketing messages by analysing customer behaviour, purchase history, and search patterns.

Outcome: This data-driven approach has enhanced the shopping experience for millions of customers and driven remarkable sales growth. Amazon's ability to cross-sell and upsell effectively is a testament to the power of integrating sales and marketing around customer insights.

Consumer Goods Pioneer: Coca-Cola

Strategy: Coca-Cola's marketing strategy creates universal appeal while allowing localised sales strategies. The company's global branding campaigns are complemented by local marketing initiatives tailored to meet consumers' unique preferences in different regions.

Outcome: This blend of global and local strategies has helped Coca-Cola maintain its position as one of the most recognisable brands worldwide while also achieving sales growth in diverse markets. The company's success highlights the importance of flexibility and customisation in sales and marketing fusion.

Lessons Learned from Industry Leaders
These case studies reveal several critical lessons for businesses seeking to integrate their sales and marketing efforts:

- **Customer-Centricity is Crucial**: Understanding and meeting customers' needs is at the heart of successful sales and marketing fusion. Leveraging customer data to inform strategies and personalise experiences can significantly enhance customer satisfaction and loyalty.

Technology Enables Alignment: Investing in technology,

such as CRM platforms and data analytics tools, facilitates collaboration between sales and marketing. These tools provide a unified view of the customer, enabling more effective targeting and engagement.

- **Flexibility and Adaptation**: It is vital to be able to adapt strategies based on market feedback and changing customer preferences. Successful companies remain agile, continuously testing and refining their approaches to stay relevant and competitive.

- **Collaboration and Communication**: Open communication and cooperation between sales and marketing teams are foundational to integration success. Regular meetings, shared goals, and cross-functional teams can bridge gaps and foster a unified approach.

These success stories demonstrate the transformative potential of sales and marketing fusion. By focusing on customer-centricity, leveraging technology, maintaining flexibility, and fostering collaboration, businesses can achieve greater efficiency, enhance customer experiences, and drive significant sales growth.

CHAPTER 11: CREATING YOUR SALES AND MARKETING FUSION PLAN

The fusion of sales and marketing is an ambitious endeavour that requires a strategic approach to ensure success. This chapter provides a roadmap for businesses looking to integrate their sales and marketing efforts effectively. From setting objectives and key performance indicators (KPIs) to implementing strategies and adapting to feedback, this guide offers a comprehensive framework for creating a sales and marketing fusion plan that drives growth and enhances customer engagement.

Setting Objectives and KPIs
Before embarking on the fusion journey, it is critical to establish clear objectives and KPIs that will guide your efforts and measure success.

- **Define Shared Objectives**: Start by defining objectives that reflect the combined goals of both sales and marketing. These include increasing overall revenue, improving lead conversion rates, or enhancing customer lifetime value.

- **Identify KPIs**: For each objective, identify specific KPIs that will enable you to measure progress. KPIs could include the number of qualified leads, conversion rates at each sales funnel stage, customer acquisition costs, and customer satisfaction scores.

- **Align Objectives with Business Goals**: Ensure that your sales and marketing objectives align with your organisation's broader goals. This alignment ensures that your efforts contribute directly to the company's success.

Implementing Your Strategies: A Step-by-Step Guide

With clear objectives and KPIs, the next step is implementing your sales and marketing fusion strategies. Here is a step-by-step guide to help you navigate this process:

1. **Collaborative Planning**: Bring together leaders and key team members from sales and marketing to develop your fusion plan collaboratively. This should include defining target customer segments, crafting unified messaging, and aligning on the customer journey.

2. **Integrate Tools and Systems**: Ensure that your CRM, marketing automation and analytics tools are integrated and accessible to both sales and marketing teams. This technological integration is crucial for sharing insights and data.

3. **Develop Joint Campaigns**: Launch marketing campaigns designed with sales input and focused on driving measurable sales outcomes. Sales teams should be equipped with marketing materials and insights to personalise their outreach.

4. **Train and Align Teams**: Conduct training sessions

to ensure sales and marketing teams understand the fusion objectives, strategies, and tools. Foster a culture of collaboration and shared responsibility for achieving goals.

5. **Execute and Monitor**: With everything in place, execute your fusion plan while closely monitoring performance against your KPIs. Ensure that there are regular check-ins where both teams can share updates, successes, and challenges.

Monitoring, Measuring, and Adapting

The final step in your sales and marketing fusion plan involves continuous monitoring, measurement, and adaptation.

- **Regular Review Sessions**: Schedule regular sessions to review progress against your KPIs, discuss what is working and what is not, and adjust strategies as needed.

- **Leverage Analytics**: Use analytics tools to gain insights into customer behaviour, campaign performance, and sales outcomes. These insights will inform your ongoing strategy and optimisation efforts.

- **Foster a Culture of Feedback**: Encourage open feedback among sales and marketing teams. Constructive feedback is vital for identifying areas for improvement and fostering innovation.

- **Adapt and Innovate**: The market and customer preferences are constantly evolving. Be prepared to adapt your strategies and explore new approaches to stay ahead of the curve and meet changing customer needs.

Creating a sales and marketing fusion plan is a dynamic process that requires commitment, collaboration, and continuous improvement. By setting clear objectives, implementing strategic actions, and being prepared to adapt based on performance and feedback, organisations can achieve a successful fusion of sales and marketing that drives growth and enhances customer relationships.

CHAPTER 12: CONCLUSION: THE PATH FORWARD

The journey towards the fusion of sales and marketing is both a strategic imperative and a transformative opportunity for businesses aiming to thrive in today's dynamic market landscape. This concluding chapter reflects on the essential steps forward, emphasising the importance of embracing change, cultivating a culture of continuous learning and improvement, and futureproofing your sales and marketing strategies.

Embracing Change in Sales and Marketing
The digital age has ushered in rapid changes in consumer behaviour, technology, and competitive landscapes, making adaptability and resilience key traits for sales and marketing teams. Businesses must embrace change not as a challenge to be feared but as an opportunity for growth and innovation. This mindset involves being proactive about integrating new technologies, staying attuned to evolving customer preferences, and being willing to experiment with new strategies. Embracing change enables organisations to remain relevant, meet customers where they are, and respond effectively to the market's ebbs and flows.

Cultivating a Culture of Continuous Learning and Improvement
The fusion of sales and marketing demands more than just

strategic alignment and technological integration; it requires a cultural shift towards continuous learning and improvement. This culture is characterised by curiosity, openness to feedback, and a commitment to professional development. Organisations can cultivate this culture by:

- **Encouraging Cross-Functional Training**: Facilitate learning opportunities for sales and marketing teams to gain insights into each other's roles, challenges, and contributions. This fosters empathy and collaboration.
- **Investing in Professional Development**: Provide access to training, conferences, and resources that keep teams current with the latest trends, tools, and methodologies in sales and marketing.
- **Promoting a Test-and-Learn Approach**: Encourage experimentation with new ideas and technologies and view failures as learning opportunities. This approach drives innovation and helps identify effective strategies more quickly.

Futureproofing Your Sales and Marketing Strategy

To ensure long-term success and competitiveness, businesses must futureproof their sales and marketing strategies. This involves anticipating future trends, understanding the potential impact of emerging technologies, and preparing for shifts in consumer behaviour. Futureproofing your strategy requires:

- **Staying Ahead of Technological Advances**: Keep abreast of developments in AI, machine learning, data analytics, and other technologies that could transform sales and marketing practices.

- **Adapting to Consumer Trends**: Continuously research and analyse consumer preferences and behaviour changes. Be ready to pivot your strategies to meet evolving customer needs.

- **Fostering Agility and Flexibility**: Build agile and flexible teams that respond quickly to market changes. Ensure your organisational structure, processes, and technology stack support rapid adaptation.

The path forward for sales and marketing fusion is one of continuous evolution, driven by a commitment to meeting customers' changing needs in innovative and effective ways. By embracing change, cultivating a culture of constant learning and improvement, and futureproofing strategies, organisations can not only navigate the complexities of today's business environment but also lay the groundwork for sustained success in the future. The fusion of sales and marketing is not the end goal but the beginning of a journey towards deeper customer engagement, enhanced collaboration, and accelerated growth.

CREDITS

To my heavenly Father, without whose blessings I wouldn't have completed a single page of this book and the books to come.

To the blessings of my parents, who are watching me from above.

I want to thank my wife, Raji, for helping me take this plunge into writing, which was and is my passion.

My mentor and friend Prakash Menon (PK as he is widely known) for telling me that I can write a book if I intend to and for giving me all the guidance I need.

Finally, my children Alen and Helen, who inspire me in everything I do.

And to everyone who helped me directly or indirectly to make this first book a reality.

A very BIG Thanks!

GLOSSARY

AI – Artificial Intelligence

AR – Augmented Reality

CRM – Customer Relationship Management

CTA – Call to Action

CAC – Customer Acquisition Cost

IoT - Internet of Things

KPI's – Key Performance Indicators

LTV – Life Time Value

ML – Machine Learning

PPC – Pay Per Click

ROI – Return on Investment

SEO – Search Engine Optimization

SEM – Search Engine Marketing

SERPs – Search Engine Result Pages

ABOUT THE AUTHOR

Shanty Abraham has been in the Enterprise sales industry for more than 3 decades in the MEA region. His love for writing started during his school days. He was always fascinated by story writers like Rudyard Kipling and R.K Narayan.

He is a God-Fearing individual and very much attached to his family. His thoughts and deeds are very secular and for him humanity is the core principle that he lives for.

Shanty is married to Raji and has two children, Alen, and Helen.

His son lives in Canada while Shanty with his wife and daughter lives in the United Arab Emirates.